WITHDRAWN

CREATIVE EDUCATION

INDIANAPOLIS COLTS

JULIE NELSON

Published by Creative Education
123 South Broad Street, Mankato, Minnesota 56001
Creative Education is an imprint of The Creative Company

Designed by Rita Marshall

Photos by: Allsport USA, Archive Photos, Bettmann/CORBIS, MBR Images,
SportsChrome

Library of Congress Cataloging-in-Publication Data

Nelson, Julie.
Indianapolis Colts / by Julie Nelson.
p. cm. — (NFL today)
Summary: Traces the history of the team from its beginnings through 1999.
ISBN 1-58341-045-7

1. Indianapolis Colts (Football team)—History—Juvenile literature. 2. Baltimore
Colts (Football team)—History—Juvenile literature. [1. Indianapolis Colts
(Football team)—History. 2. Baltimore Colts (Football team)—History.
3. Football—History.] I. Title. II. Series: NFL today (Mankato, Minn.)

GV956.I53N45   2000
796.332'64'0977252—dc21   99-015750

First edition

9 8 7 6 5 4 3 2 1

When most people think of Indianapolis, they probably think of the Indianapolis 500, perhaps the most famous auto race in the world. But there's much more to Indianapolis than just car racing.

The city has more than 700,000 citizens, making it the largest in the state of Indiana. Located in the middle of the state, Indianapolis grew from a village of 8,000 people in 1850 to the metropolis it is today. As Indianapolis has grown, so has the city's love for sports. Since 1984, Indianapolis has been home to one of the best-supported teams in the National Football League—the Indianapolis Colts.

Legendary Colts quarterback Johnny Unitas.

Defensive end Gino Marchetti played the first season of his Hall of Fame Colts career.

To get a new NFL team, most cities must settle for an expansion franchise with no history and no stars. But Indianapolis fans got a team with one of the richest traditions in the NFL. Robert Irsay, owner of the Colts, decided in 1984 that his franchise would be more successful in Indianapolis than in Baltimore, where the team had played for 30 years.

So, in the spring of 1984, moving vans appeared one evening in front of the Colts' office in Baltimore, and the club moved to Indianapolis. The team brought with it three world championships and a heritage that included some of the greatest players in football history.

UNITAS BRINGS CHAMPIONSHIP SUCCESS

The Baltimore Colts played their first season in 1953. The team was formed out of what had been the Dallas Texans in 1952. The Texans were bad, but owner Carroll Rosenbloom's wise decisions helped the Colts start to improve.

First, Rosenbloom hired Weeb Ewbank as coach for the 1954 season. Then, before the 1956 season, the Colts gave a tryout to a young quarterback named Johnny Unitas. The Baltimore coaches were impressed with Unitas's tryout and added him to the roster. In the fourth game of the 1956 season, starting quarterback George Shaw broke his leg. Unitas stepped in, led the team for the rest of the season, and established himself as a star. In 1958, the Colts won the Western Division title and earned the right to play the New York Giants in the NFL championship game.

With just under two minutes remaining in the game, the Giants led 17–14. Baltimore had the ball on its own 14-yard

Explosive wide receiver Marvin Harrison.

In only his second NFL season, Johnny Unitas passed for 24 touchdowns.

line, and few people except the Colts and Johnny Unitas believed Baltimore had a chance. As the New York fans prepared to celebrate a championship, Unitas went to work.

Unitas first completed a pass to Lenny Moore for 11 yards. Then he zeroed in on his favorite target, receiver Raymond Berry. A completion to Berry for 25 yards put the Colts at midfield. Another pass to Berry put the Colts at New York's 34-yard line. One more Unitas pass put the ball on the 13-yard line. With less than 10 seconds left, Ewbank sent in kicker Steve Myhra, who split the uprights to tie the game at 17–17. For the first time in NFL history, there would be sudden-death overtime in a championship game.

The Giants received the kickoff in overtime but soon punted to Baltimore. The Colts started from their own 20-yard line. Unitas used the running of fullback Alan Ameche and passes to Moore and Berry to move the Colts down the field. With the ball on New York's seven-yard line, Unitas gambled and threw to Berry, who caught the pass for a five-yard gain. After the game, reporters asked Unitas why he risked throwing an interception when the Colts were in sure field-goal range. "When you know what you're doing," Unitas said, "you don't throw interceptions."

On the next play, Ameche blasted into the end zone for a touchdown, giving the Colts a 23–17 victory. The Colts were world champions, and Johnny Unitas was the toast of the football world.

In 1959, the Colts won their second consecutive NFL title, beating the Giants again in the championship game, this time by a score of 31–16. Writers began calling Unitas one of the greatest quarterbacks ever to play the game. He had ability and a strong arm, but what separated him from other quarterbacks was his courage.

"You can't intimidate him," said Los Angeles Rams defensive tackle Merlin Olsen. "He waits until the last possible second to release the ball, even if it means he's going to take a good lick. When he sees us coming, he knows it's going to hurt, and we know it's going to hurt. But he just stands there and takes it. No other quarterback has such class."

Unitas led the Colts to winning season after winning season—but no championships—in the 1960s. Along the way, he continued to earn the respect and admiration of teammates and opponents alike.

"People talk about how brave Joe Namath is, and that's true, but he's no braver than John Unitas. No one is," stated Colts linebacker Mike Curtis. "John has broken about every rib in his body, and he has suffered jammed fingers and a broken nose and a broken elbow. Once he broke a rib and punctured his lung, and he had to have a tube inserted to drain the fluid from his lung. He played two weeks later."

Unitas had plenty of offensive weapons to use. Lenny Moore could run the ball or catch it, and Raymond Berry may have had the best hands of any receiver in the game. In addition, the Colts had a powerful tight end, John Mackey, who could run over tacklers once he caught the ball.

On defense, the Colts had such stars as tackle Billy Ray Smith and linebackers Don Shinnick and Dennis Gaubatz. During the 1960s, new coach Don Shula built one of the best stopping forces in football. One of the key members of that defense was Mike Curtis, a man they called "the Animal" or "Mad Dog."

1 9 5 8

Halfback Lenny Moore scored 24 points in a single game, setting a new team record.

9

Multitalented running back Eric Dickerson.

A longtime defensive leader, Duane Bickett.

Big tight end John Mackey flattened countless tacklers as he posted 644 receiving yards.

Curtis was drafted by the Colts out of Duke University in 1965. He soon became a starter for Baltimore as an outside linebacker and gained a reputation as a very hard hitter. "We were playing Green Bay," recalled Baltimore linebacker Ted Hendricks. "Jim Grabowski was coming through the line, and Mike Curtis gave him a good old-fashioned clothesline shot. He hit him so hard it popped his [Grabowski's] helmet off. Grabowski got up wobbly. One of our guys handed him his helmet. He started heading for our bench. I tapped him on the shoulder and turned him around and said, 'Yours is on the other side, Jim.'"

With Curtis wreaking havoc on the field, the Colts were again a dominant team. They won the NFL title in 1968, with Earl Morrall replacing the injured Unitas at quarterback. The Colts lost 16–7 in the Super Bowl, however, to the upstart New York Jets and Joe Namath. Two years later, the Colts were in the Super Bowl again, this time against the Dallas Cowboys. Unitas, who had led the team there, got hurt in the second quarter and was replaced by Morrall.

The Colts, who trailed 13–6 at halftime, came back to tie the game in the fourth quarter. Then it was Mike Curtis's turn to be a hero. With less than two minutes remaining in the game, Dallas quarterback Craig Morton rolled out to the right and threw downfield. The ball was tipped, and Curtis ripped it out of the air and returned it to the Dallas 28-yard line. Three plays later, Jim O'Brien kicked the game-winning field goal, and the Colts won 16–13 to claim their third world championship.

In 1971, the Colts believed they had an even better team. Curtis, who had moved to middle linebacker, was the key man in a nasty Baltimore defense that also included huge defensive lineman Bubba Smith, linebacker Ray May, and safeties Rick Volk and Jerry Logan. The Colts, who were now playing in the Eastern Division of the American Football Conference, didn't win their division in 1971. Although they did make the playoffs, they were quickly beaten by the Miami Dolphins.

As the 1972 season began, the Colts faced a rebuilding project. The team had gotten old. In addition, the Colts had a new owner, Robert Irsay, and new general manager, Joe Thomas.

One of Thomas's first moves was to trade Unitas to the San Diego Chargers after the 1972 season. Johnny Unitas's reign in Baltimore had finally come to an end. When he left

Star safety Rick Volk was one of five Baltimore defenders named to the Pro Bowl.

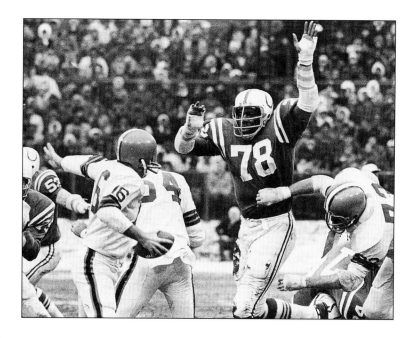

Intimidating defensive end Bubba Smith.

Baltimore, Unitas held NFL records for most pass attempts (5,110), most pass completions (2,796), most yards passing (39,768), and most touchdown passes (287). The Colts finished 5–9 in 1972, and fans in Baltimore blamed Thomas for the team's sudden decline.

Linebacker "Mad Dog" Mike Curtis brought his Colts career to a close.

JONES JAZZES UP THE COLTS

Thomas knew what the team needed: Louisiana State University quarterback Bert Jones, who had been around pro football all his life. Jones's father, Dub, had played and coached with the Cleveland Browns during the 1950s and 1960s.

Jones was the Colts' first-round draft pick in 1973. The young quarterback spent most of his time on the bench as Baltimore posted records of 4–10 in 1973 and 2–12 in 1974. Thomas knew the team needed a change, so he hired an offense-minded coach, former quarterback Ted Marchibroda, to help develop Jones.

"Ted did a mental job on me," Jones said. "We studied films, playbooks, theory, the whole thing. We even graded the other clubs we'd be playing and figured how we might attack them."

When the 1975 season began, Jones was the Colts' starter. Baltimore won its first game, but then lost four in a row. In the next game, the Colts trailed the New York Jets 21–0 at halftime. Marchibroda stuck with Jones, and the Colts scored six touchdowns in the second half to win 45–28. The Colts kept on winning, too. In the final two games of the regular season, Jones engineered comeback victories over Miami

Quarterback Bert Jones was a fearless leader.

The Colts' all-time leading rusher, Lydell Mitchell.

and New England. The Colts, who had started the season with a 1–4 record, won nine games in a row to finish 10–4 and claimed the team's first division title in five years. Although Baltimore lost to Pittsburgh in the first round of the playoffs, the future looked very bright. In addition to Jones, the Colts had stars in running back Lydell Mitchell and tight end Raymond Chester.

Jones's leadership earned the respect of his teammates. Before a game in 1976 against the Houston Oilers, Jones had a bad case of the flu. But he played anyway and led the Colts to victory. "He was so sick yesterday that I thought he'd fall down if an Oiler so much as breathed on him," said offensive lineman George Kunz the next day. "But he played another great game. He's tough. . . . It kind of rubs off on the rest of us."

Jones and the Colts won the AFC East in 1976 and 1977 but lost in the first round of the playoffs both times. The winning ways didn't last, however. Mitchell was traded to San Diego in 1978, and Jones was often injured. Marchibroda was fired after the team went 5–11 during the 1979 season. The Colts had risen to the top very quickly under Jones; unfortunately, they fell to the bottom just as quickly. Baltimore, wanting to build for the future, traded Jones to the Los Angeles Rams in 1981.

The "Baltimore" Colts never had another winning season. After the team went 7–9 in 1983, Irsay decided he had had enough of Baltimore. Investors from Indianapolis talked Irsay into moving the team to their city. It wasn't a tough sell. Indianapolis had just finished building the 60,000-seat Hoosier Dome, a beautiful indoor stadium.

1 9 8 3

Massive offensive lineman Chris Hinton played the first of seven seasons with the Colts.

Speedy kick returner Clarence Verdin (pages 18-19).

17

Duane Bickett led a Colts defense that gave up just 15 points per game.

The Colts had a new home, but they were still losers. Frank Kush, a defense-minded coach, was replaced by Rod Dowhower, but the team didn't have enough talent to compete for a championship. In 1986, Indianapolis lost its first 13 games. General manager Jim Irsay, son of the owner, then fired Dowhower and named Ron Meyer as the new coach. Meyer had an immediate impact, and the Colts won their last three games of the 1986 season. Suddenly, hopes were high for 1987.

THE DICKERSON YEARS

The Colts were an improved team in 1987, but Irsay found a way to make the team much better with the addition of just one player: the best running back in the NFL.

No runner in league history had as quick a rise to the top as Eric Dickerson. Drafted by the Los Angeles Rams in 1983, Dickerson led the NFL in rushing his rookie year with 1,808 yards. By 1987, though, Dickerson no longer wanted to play for Los Angeles. He felt he should be paid more, but the Rams refused to rewrite his contract. Finally, Dickerson told the Rams to trade him.

The trade was made in early November 1987. When Dickerson joined the Colts, Meyer already had the team believing it could win. Running back Albert Bentley was a solid runner and pass catcher, and receiver Bill Brooks was a deep threat. But the best part of the Colts offense was the line: center Ray Donaldson, guard Ron Solt, and tackle Chris Hinton were all Pro-Bowl players. On defense, linebacker Duane Bickett led the team in sacks and was also a Pro-Bowl pick.

All of this talent combined to lead the Colts to a 9–6 record in 1987, which was good enough to win the AFC Eastern Division title. The Colts had made it to the playoffs for the first time in 10 years, but they lost in the first round to Cleveland, 38–21.

In 1988, Indianapolis picked up two key additions. The team obtained linebacker Fredd Young in a trade with the Seattle Seahawks. It also drafted a quarterback, Chris Chandler, who had an immediate impact as a rookie, leading the team to a 9–7 record. Unfortunately, that wasn't good enough to qualify for postseason play. The following year, injuries sidelined Chandler and Dickerson. Veteran quarterback Jack Trudeau filled in for Chandler, but he couldn't lead the hurting Colts to the playoffs.

Tough All-Pro center Ray Donaldson anchored the Colts' offensive line for the 10th season.

Hard-working halfback Eric Dickerson.

Marshall Faulk combined great vision and incredible acceleration.

In 1990, the Colts traded Hinton and wide receiver Andre Rison, as well as draft choices, to the Atlanta Falcons for the first pick in the NFL draft. The Colts then selected University of Illinois quarterback Jeff George and signed him to a $15-million contract.

George enjoyed a solid rookie season in 1990, throwing 16 touchdown passes. But the veteran Dickerson was now on the downside of his career, and the Colts lacked a strong running game to balance the offense. The Colts finished 7–9 that year, then plummeted to an embarrassing 1–15 in 1991. The once-mighty Colts had reached a new low point.

1 9 9 0

In his rookie season, strong-armed quarterback Jeff George passed for 2,152 yards.

MARCHIBRODA'S COLTS

It was time to rebuild—starting with a new head coach. Ted Marchibroda, who had made the Colts winners in Baltimore in the mid-1970s, was hired again in 1992 to do the same in Indianapolis. In training camp, Marchibroda set a standard of dedication that impressed his players. Coaching, he believed, was "a 24-hour-a-day job. No motivating speech is going to make the difference. You have to work with your football team every minute to get it ready to play on Sunday."

Marchibroda's leadership paid off. With a 9–7 record, the 1992 Colts tied the all-time NFL mark for the best turnaround in a single NFL season—posting eight wins more than the previous year. But the team slumped to 4–12 the following season, and George was traded to the Atlanta Falcons. Marchibroda needed immediate help both at running back and at quarterback.

23

The first need was taken care of when the Colts made San Diego State running back Marshall Faulk their number one pick in the 1994 NFL draft. Faulk rushed for more than 100 yards in his first two games and went on to become the NFL Offensive Rookie of the Year.

Clearly, the Colts had found their running back. But filling the quarterback position wasn't as easy. Jim Harbaugh, who had spent seven years with the Chicago Bears, was signed as a free agent in 1994.

Though he struggled in his first season, Harbaugh rebounded in 1995, passing for 17 touchdowns and leading Indianapolis to a 9–7 record. In the playoffs, the "Cinderella" Colts upset the defending AFC champion San Diego Chargers 35–20 and the powerful Kansas City Chiefs 10–7.

1 9 9 6

Safety Jason Belser added to the Colts' offense by scoring two touchdowns on interceptions.

Kick returner Aaron Bailey.

The following week, in a memorable AFC championship game, the Colts were narrowly defeated by the Pittsburgh Steelers, 20–16. The outcome came down to the final play, when Harbaugh lofted a "Hail Mary" pass from the Pittsburgh 29-yard line into the right corner of the end zone. Despite the frantic efforts of the Steelers defenders to bat away the football, Colts receiver Aaron Bailey almost came up with it as he fell to the ground. Instead, the ball bounced off his hip, and Pittsburgh held on for the hard-fought win.

Placekicker Cary Blanchard made 32 field goals, the second-highest total in the league.

The Colts continued to play well in 1996. Under new head coach Lindy Infante, the team finished 9–7 and qualified for another playoff berth, the team's first back-to-back playoff appearances in nearly 20 years.

Harbaugh continued to lead the offense at quarterback, connecting with new Colts receiver Marvin Harrison for 836 yards, and Faulk again led Indianapolis on the ground. But perhaps the player with the most success in 1996 was kicker Cary Blanchard, who led the league in field goal percentage (.900), earned Pro-Bowl election, and was named the NFL Kicker of the Year. In spite of the impressive individual performances, the season ended on a sour note with a 42–14 playoff loss to Pittsburgh.

That disappointment marked the beginning of a downward spiral for Indianapolis. The Colts finished 3–13 in 1997 after losing their first 10 games of the season. The lone bright spot of the season came on November 16, when Indianapolis pulled off an upset over the defending Super Bowl champions, the Green Bay Packers. Blanchard booted a 20-yard field goal at the gun as the Colts downed Green Bay 41–38 in a wild shootout at the RCA Dome in Indianapolis.

Star quarterback Peyton Manning (pages 26-27).

Jim Mora was hired as the new head coach of the Indianapolis Colts on January 12.

In 1998, the Colts brought in a new coach, a new president, and a new quarterback. Jim Mora, who had coached the New Orleans Saints to four playoff berths in 10 seasons, was named the new head coach of the Colts in January 1998. He was hired by Bill Polian, the new president of the Indianapolis franchise.

Mora and Polian immediately had a major decision to make in the 1998 NFL draft. The Colts owned the draft's top overall pick, and the team—which had just traded Jim Harbaugh to the new Ravens franchise in Baltimore—sorely needed a quarterback. The two top college quarterbacks available were Peyton Manning of Tennessee and Ryan Leaf of Washington State.

The Colts opted for Manning, a decision that paid off immediately. While Leaf struggled with the San Diego Chargers in his rookie season, Manning's strong play eased the pain of another 3–13 season in 1998. "He's the kind of guy who wants to be coached," Mora explained. "You can't overwork him. He's like a sponge. He wants to do the best he can, and he wants you to give him all that you have to give him."

The son of former New Orleans Saints quarterback Archie Manning, Peyton had graduated with academic honors in only three years at the University of Tennessee. Peyton was so popular among the Tennessee faithful that, shortly after he decided to return for his senior season to again quarterback the Volunteers, several newborn babies in the area—as well as a baby giraffe at a local zoo—were given the name "Peyton" in his honor.

Though the Colts struggled for wins in 1998, Manning rewrote the NFL rookie record books and set several franchise marks. The young quarterback set a Colts single-season record for total passing yards with 3,739, breaking not only the rookie mark, but also that of legendary Colts quarterback Johnny Unitas. Manning also set records for most passing attempts (575) and most completions (326). Still, there were obvious indications that he was a rookie, as he set another team record by throwing 28 interceptions.

Manning's transition to the professional ranks was made easier by the reliable Marshall Faulk, who led the team in both rushing and receiving yards. But Faulk's days in Indianapolis ended there. After the season, he was traded to St. Louis for two draft picks. The Colts then selected running back Edgerrin James of Miami in the 1999 NFL draft.

Though most experts had pegged Heisman Trophy winner Ricky Williams as the draft's top running back, Coach Mora liked what he saw in James. "Edgerrin has a great work ethic and prepares well," Mora said. "He spends a lot of time in his playbook, and he really wants to be a good football player."

Indianapolis built on to its defense as well by signing several free agents, including defensive ends Chad Bratzke and Shawn King and linebacker Cornelius Bennett. "There is no long-term thinking here," Manning explained. "This team wants to win right now."

And win the Colts did, rebounding from their 3–13 season by going 13–3 and capturing the championship of the powerful AFC Eastern Conference. Along the way, the Colts compiled an 11-game winning streak behind three of the league's

1 9 9 9

Veteran linebacker Cornelius Bennett played his first season in Indianapolis, making 102 tackles.

29

Backfield sensation Edgerrin James.

End Chad Bratzke spearheaded the Colts' pass rush.

brightest young offensive stars: James, who led the NFL in rushing with 1,553 yards and 13 touchdowns; Marvin Harrison, who led all receivers with 1,663 yards and 12 touchdowns; and Manning, who threw for more than 4,000 yards.

Indianapolis received a playoff bye before taking on the Tennessee Titans. Unfortunately, the young Colts struggled against the Titans' stingy defense, scoring only three field goals until less than two minutes remained in the game. A touchdown run by Manning late in the fourth quarter was too little too late for the Colts, and Tennessee prevailed 19–16.

Indianapolis fans were disappointed, but the mood in the Colts locker room remained upbeat. "We'll try to reload a little," Manning said after the game, "[but] I'm confident we can get right back here next season."

With an offense featuring Manning, Harrison, and James, the Colts should remain a powerhouse in the AFC for years to come. Fans hope that the team's dramatic rebirth in 1999 will lead to the franchise's fifth world championship—and a new era of greatness in the 21st century.

2 0 0 1

Powerful linebacker Mike Peterson was expected to be a defensive leader.